Speak Out Loud

Mastering the Art of Public Speaking

by Richard Bell

Formatted, Converted, and Distributed by eBookIt.com
http://www.eBookIt.com

ISBN-13: 9781456641474 (paperback)
ISBN-13: 9781456641467 (ebook)
ISBN-13: 9781456641481 (audiobook)

Dear Esteemed Reader,

Thank you immensely for choosing this book to join your collection. We imagine that you've already embarked on an exploration of ideas within these pages, and we couldn't be happier about it!

Now, if you find yourself chuckling, pondering, or even debating with the words in front of you, we'd absolutely love to hear about it. If you can spare a few moments to pen down your thoughts in a review, we would be as delighted as a dictionary on a spelling bee!

An Amazon review would be excellent - but hey, we're far from picky. Whether it's a scribble on the back of a grocery list, a tweet, or even a message in a bottle (though that might take a while to reach us), your feedback is gold.

Writing a review might not be as fun as a spontaneous dance-off, but we promise it'll bring grins to our faces, warmth to our hearts, and incredibly valuable insights to future readers.

With Gratitude,

Bo Bennett, PhD
Publisher
Archieboy Holdings, LLC.

Table of Contents

Introduction

The Power of Public Speaking

Picture yourself standing on a stage, a sea of expectant faces gazing at you, ready to absorb your every word. There's an electrifying power at your disposal in this moment: the power of public speaking. It's an art that has been harnessed since the dawn of civilization, molding the world and transforming individuals into leaders and influencers. Public speaking has been the medium through which ideas have been spread, innovations have been initiated, and revolutions have been instigated. This power is not reserved for a select few; it is accessible to anyone who dares to learn and master it.

Through public speaking, you can influence your audience's opinions, motivate them to take action, or simply entertain them. Whether you're presenting an innovative idea to a group of colleagues, making a best man's speech at your friend's wedding, or standing in front of hundreds at a conference, the ability to express your ideas convincingly is invaluable. The words you speak and the way you deliver them can have a transformative effect on your listeners.

Public speaking is not just about talking in front of people. It's about engaging with your audience, persuading them, informing them, and even entertaining them. It requires clarity of thought, an understanding of the audience's needs and expectations, and the ability to adapt your message to make the most impact.

Public speaking isn't just beneficial in terms of external communication; it can also bring about personal growth. As you become more comfortable with public speaking, you can experience a boost in self-confidence, improved critical thinking, enhanced leadership skills, and superior interpersonal communication. It's a tool for self-improvement, a vehicle for personal growth.

This section is about understanding and appreciating the inherent power of public speaking, exploring its benefits, and igniting your desire to harness it. By comprehending this power, you'll be eager to dive into the following sections, where we delve into the nuances of this art and science. So, let's embark on this journey, and explore the exceptional power of public speaking.

Who Should Read This Book?

Let's get one thing straight right from the start: public speaking is not a skill reserved only for the charismatic or the eloquent. It is a craft that can be honed by anyone willing to learn and practice. So, who should read this book? Short answer: anyone who has something to say.

If you're a student needing to present your research findings, this book will provide you with the tools to structure your presentation and deliver it confidently. Are you a business professional aiming to motivate your team or pitch to potential investors? This book will help you hone your persuasive skills to achieve your objectives. If you are an educator looking to inspire your students, the principles and strategies discussed here will allow you to engage your listeners effectively.

Perhaps you're a nervous best man who must deliver a memorable toast at a wedding or an introverted author having to promote a book in public? The insights in this book will guide you in overcoming the anxiety associated with public speaking and help you command attention with your words.

This book is also for the experienced speakers who wish to refine their skills further, aiming to turn good into great. The advanced strategies discussed in the later sections will provide that extra edge, the minute refinements that can make a significant difference.

If you're someone who believes in the power of ideas, in the ability of words to inspire change, then this book is definitely for you. Because this book is about empowering you to share your ideas, your stories, and your insights with the world in the most impactful way possible - through the art of public speaking. No matter where you stand today, with persistence and the right guidance, you can master this art. So, shall we begin this journey together?

Chapter 1:
The Anatomy of Fear

Think back to a time when you were asked to give a speech. Your heart might have begun to race, your palms may have turned clammy, and your mind might have filled with a whirlwind of fear and doubt. These reactions, my friends, are perfectly normal. You see, public speaking is considered one of the most common fears worldwide, often ranked higher than the fear of death itself!

In this chapter, we're going to be diving headfirst into the heart of that fear. We're not just going to examine it, but dissect it, understand it, and find ways to transform it. We'll start by understanding what speech anxiety is and what triggers it. We'll explore the psychological and physiological responses it induces, helping you recognize the signs and symptoms.

Then, we'll venture into the heart of fear, unearthing strategies to harness that fear and turn it into a source of energy and motivation. We'll take the stage not in spite of fear, but with it, allowing it to fuel our performance rather than hinder it. By the end of this chapter, you'll be well-equipped to confront your speech anxiety head-on and channel it productively to electrify your public speaking performances. So, take a deep breath, and let's step into the spotlight.

Understanding Speech Anxiety

Speech anxiety - the looming specter for many a potential speaker - is not as invincible as it first appears. Indeed, the first step to triumphing over speech anxiety is understanding it. So, let's start by uncovering what it actually is. Speech anxiety, also known as *glossophobia,* is the fear of public speaking. It's a form of social anxiety where one fears judgement, embarrassment, or humiliation while speaking in front of others.

If the mere thought of public speaking makes your palms sweat and your heart pound, know that you're not alone. Surveys indicate that as much as 75% of the population experiences some degree of anxiety or nervousness when it comes to public speaking. The physical symptoms are real, and they can be overwhelming: trembling hands, shaky voice, racing pulse, dry mouth, tight throat - these are all common manifestations of speech anxiety.

But have you ever wondered why we experience these symptoms in the first place?

At its core, speech anxiety is a primal response. Our brains are wired to alert us to potential threats in our environment, a holdover from our early ancestors who needed to be on constant alert for predators. When we're the center of attention in a public speaking situation, our brain perceives the audience as a potential threat. This perception triggers a "fight or flight" response, releasing a flood of adrenaline into our systems, which in turn causes the physical symptoms associated with anxiety.

But understanding is only the beginning. The real magic happens when we begin to reframe this understanding and utilize it to our advantage. We'll start to see that our fear doesn't have to be our enemy. Instead, it can serve as a source of strength, providing us with the energy and focus we need to deliver powerful, impactful speeches. But to tap into this strength, we need to move from fear to courage, turning our nerves into a wellspring of energy that can fuel our performance rather than hinder it. We'll tackle this in the next section, turning the spotlight onto the journey from fear to courage.

From Fear to Courage: Turning Nerves into Energy

Having dissected the nature of speech anxiety, it's time to address the real question: how do we journey from fear to courage? The secret lies in our understanding of fear, not as an insurmountable wall but as a hurdle we can leap over with the right strategies. The adrenaline surge that we experience when we're anxious about public speaking, while initially seen as the enemy, can actually be the untapped source of energy we need to engage and captivate our audience.

First, we need to reconsider our relationship with fear. As we have already established, it's a primal response to perceived danger, and it's perfectly normal to feel this way when you're standing in front of a crowd. However, this doesn't mean that we should let fear dictate our actions. Instead of viewing the fear as an obstacle, consider it as an indication that you're pushing yourself out of your comfort zone. Fear doesn't mean 'stop,' it means 'proceed with caution.' Embrace this mindset, and you'll find your fear start to lose its hold on you.

Next, comes the process of transforming our nervous energy into productive energy. One of the most potent ways to achieve this is through visualization. This is not a mystical concept but a psychological tool used by athletes, performers, and yes, successful public speakers. By mentally rehearsing your speech and visualizing a successful delivery, you begin to build a cognitive blueprint for success. Visualize the audience's positive reactions, their applause, their engagement, and you'll start to associate public speaking with positive outcomes rather than negative ones.

Another invaluable tool in your arsenal is controlled breathing. When we're anxious, our breath becomes shallow, which can exacerbate feelings of anxiety. By learning to control your breathing, you can not only counteract this effect but also tap into a natural way to calm your nerves. Deep, controlled breathing can help to lower your heart rate, stabilize your blood pressure, and provide a sense of calm and control.

Lastly, don't underestimate the power of preparation. Familiarity breeds confidence, and the more familiar you are with your material, the less room there is for anxiety to creep in. Practice, practice, practice until you feel like you could deliver your speech in your sleep. Then practice some more.

Ultimately, the journey from fear to courage is deeply personal and unique to each individual. It's not about eradicating fear altogether but learning to harness it, turning nerves into energy that can fuel your public speaking performance. Remember, fear isn't a sign of weakness, but a sign that you're about to do something brave. So, embrace your fear, turn it into courage, and let it propel you to new heights in your public speaking journey. The path ahead will have more tools and techniques to help you do just that. So, hang tight, and prepare for an adventure of self-discovery and growth.

Chapter 2: Your Voice, Your Identity

In the grand theater of public speaking, the voice is a pivotal actor. As you move forward from understanding and addressing the fear of public speaking, you are now ready to explore the power and intricacies of your voice. Our focus in this chapter is twofold. First, we will delve into the significant role your voice plays in public speaking, underscoring its importance in conveying your messages effectively. Next, we venture into the process of discovering and honing your unique, authentic voice, a critical component that distinguishes you from others and fortifies your identity as a speaker. Together, these sections will guide you to better understand and harness the potential of your voice, propelling you to be the master of your own message. Let's embark on this exciting journey of voice and identity.

The Importance of Voice in Public Speaking

There is a powerful and often under-appreciated tool in our public speaking arsenal, one that can enchant an audience or send them into a somnolent stupor. That tool is your voice. It's the vehicle that carries your words, emotions, and personality across the auditorium or conference room. Imagine your speech as a finely crafted ship, meticulously designed and well-prepared for its voyage. Your voice is the sea on which this ship sails; too placid and your audience may lose interest, too stormy and your message might get lost in the waves. Striking the perfect balance ensures your audience is engaged and your message resonates.

Now, to understand the importance of voice in public speaking, let's first separate the concept of voice into two categories: physical and personal. The physical aspect of your voice encompasses the quality, tone, volume, pace, and inflection. These are the auditory characteristics that can either captivate your audience or potentially drive them to distraction. On the other hand, your personal voice is about your unique style, your authenticity, the way you use words and construct sentences—it's a reflection of your personality. Together, these two aspects of voice play a decisive role in how your message is received.

There's a reason people often comment on a speaker's voice after a speech, whether it's about how soothing it was, how dynamic, or maybe even how monotonous. The sound of your voice and the way you use it can significantly affect your audience's perception and their engagement. A well-modulated voice can make even the most mundane topic seem intriguing, while a monotone delivery can make even the most riveting subject sound uninteresting.

Furthermore, your voice can subconsciously communicate your confidence, enthusiasm, or nervousness to your audience. Remember, the audience doesn't only listen to your words; they 'hear' your feelings and attitudes as well. By mastering your voice, you take control of the subtext of your speech and can more effectively steer audience reactions.

In addition, your personal voice—your unique style of expressing thoughts—can help establish a deeper connection with your audience. It can make you more relatable and trustworthy, and thus, your message more persuasive. When you communicate with authenticity, your audience is more likely to listen and respond positively.

In summary, your voice, in its physical and personal aspects, is a powerful tool in public speaking. It can influence your audience's attention, comprehension, retention, and overall perception of you and your message. By understanding and harnessing the power of your voice, you can turn your speeches into memorable experiences that engage, inspire, and resonate with your listeners. It's time to make your voice heard!

Finding and Refining Your Authentic Voice

Discovering your authentic voice is akin to unearthing a hidden gem. It's something deeply personal, unique, and valuable. But, like any uncut gem, it often needs refining to truly shine. Your authentic voice is not about putting on a performance or mimicking someone else; rather, it's about embracing and accentuating your individuality in your speeches. Let's delve into how you can uncover and polish your authentic voice for public speaking.

The first step to finding your authentic voice is self-reflection. Consider your values, your passions, your experiences. What messages are you passionate about sharing? What communication style feels most natural to you? Your authentic voice should be a reflection of who you are and what you stand for. It may be helpful to jot down some key words or phrases that you feel represent you and your speaking style.

Next, it's crucial to cultivate self-awareness about your current speaking habits. Listen to recordings of yourself speaking, and pay attention to your pacing, volume, tone, and the natural rhythms and inflections of your speech. Notice how you naturally emphasize certain words or alter your tone to convey different emotions. This exercise can help you understand how you naturally communicate and identify areas that may need refining.

To refine your authentic voice, consider aspects such as pacing, volume, and tone. A slower pace can allow your audience to absorb your message more fully, while a faster pace can convey excitement or urgency. Adjusting your volume can help you emphasize key points and hold your audience's attention. Your tone of voice can communicate a range of emotions and attitudes, enhancing your words' impact. Experiment with these elements in different combinations to discover what feels most natural and effective for you.

Alongside these technical aspects, also focus on your word choices and storytelling style. Do you prefer using simple language or more complex expressions? Do you engage your audience with personal anecdotes or rely on data and research? Your choice of words and the way you structure your speech contribute significantly to your personal voice.

It's also essential to remain open to feedback and continuously refine your voice. Seeking feedback from trusted friends, colleagues, or mentors can provide valuable insights into how your voice is perceived and how effectively it communicates your intended message.

Above all, remember that finding and refining your voice is a process. It's about embracing your unique style and making conscious choices to enhance your natural communication strengths. Over time, with practice and perseverance, you will develop an authentic voice that truly reflects you and resonates with your audience. Be patient with yourself, trust the process, and remember that every step you take brings you closer to the compelling, authentic public speaker you aspire to be.

Chapter 3:
Know Your Audience

Have you ever wondered why some speeches strike a chord while others seem to fall on deaf ears? A primary factor is the speaker's understanding of their audience. In this chapter, we're going to dive into the psychology of the audience. It's not enough to master your fear and find your voice if you don't know who you're talking to or what they expect. We start this chapter with a deep dive into understanding audience expectations, because grasping these is as critical as getting your content right. Following that, we'll discuss the art of tailoring your message to your audience, an exercise that involves a blend of empathy, understanding, and strategic thinking. This chapter will show you how to become an audience-focused speaker, a skill that will make your speeches more impactful and memorable. So let's set our sights on the people in the chairs, because public speaking isn't a monologue, it's a dialogue.

Understanding Audience Expectations

When you're preparing a speech, you might wonder, "What does my audience expect from me?" It's a common question and a vital one. From the moment you step onto the stage, the audience has expectations. They might expect to learn something new, be entertained, inspired, persuaded, or simply feel included in the conversation. The ability to gauge these expectations and fulfill them is what separates a good speaker from a great one.

Before even putting pen to paper or fingers to keys, understanding your audience is paramount. Let's begin by identifying who makes up your audience. This involves not only demographic factors such as age, education, and cultural background but also their prior knowledge and experience related to your topic. This information is instrumental in shaping your language, tone, and content.

Next, we delve into the psychographics of your audience. Are they here voluntarily, or is attendance mandatory? What are their values, beliefs, and attitudes towards your subject? Understanding these aspects helps you form a connection with your audience, making your speech more impactful.

Keep in mind, audience expectations also depend on the context of the speech. A toast at a wedding will differ greatly from a presentation in a business meeting. The former might expect sentiment and humor, while the latter looks for value and actionable insights. Always take into account the setting and purpose of your speech.

Now, let's talk about the unstated yet omnipresent expectation: to be engaged. Regardless of why they're in the audience, every listener wants to be engaged. This means your speech must be informative, compelling, and perhaps even entertaining. A bored audience is unlikely to take away anything meaningful from your speech, regardless of how important the content might be.

In addition, the audience expects you to respect their time. This means keeping to your allotted time, avoiding unnecessary repetition, and maintaining a clear, focused message. Time management is a clear indication of your respect for the audience's time and attention.

Lastly, never underestimate the audience's expectation of authenticity. In an age where information is abundant, authenticity is scarce and thus, highly valued. The audience expects you to be sincere, genuine, and trustworthy.

Your authenticity can make even the most complex or mundane subjects resonate with the audience.

In conclusion, understanding your audience's expectations is a complex task, with several layers of consideration. But, as you'll soon find, it's an exercise that holds the key to delivering a speech that resonates, influences, and inspires. In the following section, we'll explore how you can tailor your message to suit these diverse expectations, truly hitting the mark with your audience.

Tailoring Your Message to Your Audience

Having spent time understanding your audience's expectations, let's now delve into how you can tailor your message to meet these expectations effectively. Tailoring your message doesn't mean manipulating your speech to tell the audience what they want to hear. It's about respecting the audience's intellect, interests, and time, and delivering a message that resonates with them on a deeper level.

Firstly, structure your content wisely. The information should flow in a logical and compelling manner, keeping the audience engaged from start to finish. If your speech is a journey, think of the audience as your passengers - they need clear signs, interesting sights, and a sense of where they are headed.

Next, consider the language you use. An audience of industry professionals may appreciate jargon, while a more general audience will require simpler, more accessible language. The use of inclusive language – language that avoids bias, slang, or references that could exclude members of your audience – is also crucial. It's not just about what you say, but how you say it.

Humor is another useful tool in tailoring your message. However, it's like hot sauce - a little can enhance the meal, too much can ruin it. Gauge your audience's receptivity to humor. Anecdotes, light-hearted observations, or amusing facts relevant to your speech can make your presentation more engaging and relatable.

One important aspect of tailoring your message is making it relevant to your audience. This requires some effort to understand their needs, desires, and challenges. By addressing these factors, you're not just delivering a speech; you're providing value, which heightens audience engagement.

Speaking of value, concrete examples and case studies enhance your message's impact by bringing abstract concepts to life. By relating your points to real-world scenarios that your audience can relate to, you make your message both engaging and memorable.

Visual aids can also be very effective when used appropriately. Whether it's a simple PowerPoint presentation or sophisticated multimedia, visual aids can help communicate complex ideas, add visual interest and provide a shared focus for the audience.

Moreover, ask for audience participation when appropriate. This can be in the form of questions, group discussions, or even hands-on activities. Such involvement can make the audience feel invested in your presentation, making your message more impactful.

Lastly, always leave room for flexibility. Despite your best preparations, you might find the audience's response differing from your expectations. In such situations, being able to adapt your message on the fly is a skill that will stand you in good stead.

In conclusion, tailoring your message to your audience is both an art and a science. It requires understanding your audience, using appropriate language and tools, and always staying flexible. A well-tailored message will not only satisfy audience expectations but may even exceed them, making your speech an unforgettable experience. As we journey forward, we'll explore how nonverbal communication can complement your tailored message, adding another dimension to your public speaking skills.

Chapter 4:
The Power of Nonverbal Communication

As we delve into the fascinating world of nonverbal communication, you'll learn just how crucial it is in the realm of public speaking. The words we utter form only a fraction of our communication. The rest is communicated through our body language, facial expressions, gestures, and posture, which collectively hold immense power to reinforce, complement, or even contradict the message we convey verbally. In this chapter, we will first dissect the role of body language in public speaking, understanding its nuances and impact. Then, we will guide you through mastering the use of facial expressions, gestures, and posture to your advantage. By the end of this chapter, you'll have added a new layer of skill to your public speaking arsenal - one that silently yet profoundly influences your audience's perception and response.

Body Language and Its Role in Public Speaking

While words express our thoughts, it is our body language that provides a window to our emotions, beliefs, and attitudes. As a public speaker, it's essential to understand the impact of body language on your presentation and learn how to harness it effectively to accentuate your verbal message.

Think about body language as the silent singer of your thoughts. It can underline your words, giving them extra emphasis. It can provide an unspoken commentary, adding depth to your narrative. Or it can signal confidence and credibility, persuading your audience before you've uttered a single word. Body language is indeed a powerful tool when wielded correctly.

Just as it can enhance your speech, improper body language can undermine it. Unwanted signals such as crossing arms, lack of eye contact, or fidgeting can generate a negative impression, distracting your audience from the content of your speech. Therefore, mastering body language is about not only using it to emphasize your message but also controlling it to avoid miscommunication.

Remember that body language can be both conscious and unconscious. While you may be focusing on delivering your speech, your body could be telling its own story, revealing your underlying emotions and attitudes. This unconscious communication can often be more truthful than words, and your audience will pick up on these subtle cues. Thus, aligning your verbal and nonverbal communication is crucial for a successful speech.

A strong understanding of body language starts with self-awareness. Observing yourself, perhaps through video recordings, can help you recognize your natural body language tendencies. Once you're familiar with these, you can work on modifying them to suit your speaking style and to ensure they're reinforcing, not contradicting, your verbal message.

Next comes the art of reading others. Being able to interpret your audience's body language allows you to adapt your speech in real-time, ensuring you maintain their interest and address their reactions.

Lastly, think of body language as an orchestra, with each element playing its part to create a harmonious whole. Your posture, facial expressions, gestures, and movement all contribute to your overall body language. We will delve deeper into these in the following sections.

In sum, body language in public speaking is like the frame around a painting - it enhances the picture, focuses attention, and complements the work. Master it, and you'll not only amplify your message but also gain an extra level of connection with your audience, making your speech truly unforgettable.

Facial Expressions, Gestures, and Posture: Making Them Work For You

As the idiom goes, 'actions speak louder than words', and in public speaking, your facial expressions, gestures, and posture can indeed amplify, modify, or even contradict your verbal message. Let's take a closer look at these nonverbal cues and see how they can work for you.

Let's start with facial expressions. Your face is like a billboard displaying your emotions. A warm smile can create an immediate connection, while raised eyebrows can indicate surprise or curiosity. A frown might suggest confusion or disagreement. Being aware of these subtle signals can help you manage how your audience perceives you. But remember, authenticity is key. People are generally good at detecting fake expressions, so make sure your facial cues align with your feelings and words.

Gestures, on the other hand, are the accents of your verbal language. They can highlight key points, describe something, or convey a particular emotion. For example, you might use your hands to show the size or shape of an object, or point to direct your audience's attention. Gestures should be natural and varied, but be careful not to overdo them. Excessive or repetitive movements can become a distraction.

Posture, the silent broadcaster of your confidence and credibility, often goes unnoticed by speakers, yet it significantly impacts the audience's perception. An upright, open posture can project confidence and authority, while slouching or leaning can give an impression of nervousness or disinterest. Be mindful of maintaining a strong, stable, and relaxed stance. Keep your shoulders relaxed, feet firmly grounded, and remember that the aim is not to freeze in a rigid posture but to move naturally and purposefully.

Think of these nonverbal elements as different instruments in your communication orchestra. Each plays a vital role, but they must be in harmony to produce the most impactful performance. A mismatch, such as saying something positive with a frown, can lead to confusion or disbelief.

Here's a piece of practical advice. Use a mirror or record yourself while practicing your speech. This can help you become more aware of your expressions, gestures, and posture. Watch the recording critically, identify any habits that might detract from your message, and work to change them.

Lastly, remember to practice 'active rest'. This is a state where you're still and quiet but fully present and connected with your audience. Avoid unnecessary fidgeting or shuffling, which can distract your listeners.

Mastering facial expressions, gestures, and posture requires time, practice, and most importantly, self-awareness. With persistence, these nonverbal cues can become your secret weapon, helping you deliver a powerful, memorable speech that resonates with your audience.

Chapter 5: Mastering Verbal Communication

As we step into the domain of verbal communication, we are greeted with an arsenal of powerful tools. However, it's not just about wielding these tools, but knowing how to use them effectively to drive home your message. In this chapter, we will navigate through the nuances of language choice—how the clarity, brevity, and impact of your words can make a lasting impression on your audience. But remember, public speaking isn't a monologue. It's a dialogue between you and your audience, woven with the vibrant threads of storytelling. Therefore, we will also delve into the art of storytelling in public speaking—understanding its power, mastering its techniques, and learning to weave your narrative into your speech to captivate and connect with your audience on a deeper level. Let's step into the magic of words and the narratives they can spin. Let's master verbal communication.

Language Choice: Clarity, Brevity, and Impact

Remember when you were a kid, sitting cross-legged on the floor as your parents read you a bedtime story? The words they used—clear, simple, and impactful—formed vivid images in your mind, brought characters to life, and made the story engaging. As grown-ups in the world of public speaking, we still need to tell our stories in a way that is clear, concise, and impactful.

Let's start with clarity. When crafting your speech, it is essential to select words that accurately convey your message. Don't make your audience work to understand you; instead, make your message so clear that it's almost impossible to be misunderstood. To do this, you need to avoid jargon and overly complex language. Instead, use everyday words that your audience is familiar with. When it comes to clarity, remember this: If your grandmother wouldn't understand it, your audience might not either.

Now, let's turn to brevity. Have you ever listened to a speaker who seemed to be in love with their own voice, meandering around the point and overstuffing their sentences with unnecessary words? Don't be that person. Your audience is there to hear your message, not marvel at your extensive vocabulary. Trim the fat from your speech. Be concise, be on point, and get your message across without testing your audience's patience.

And finally, we arrive at impact. The impact of your words hinges on your choice of language. Words have power—they can inspire, provoke, comfort, and drive people to action. Carefully chosen words can make your message resonate with your audience and make it memorable. To create an impact, opt for strong, evocative words that pack a punch. Use vivid language that appeals to the senses and emotions. And remember, sometimes, silence can be the most powerful 'word' of all.

In the world of public speaking, your words are your currency. Invest in clarity to be understood, in brevity to be appreciated, and in impactful words to be remembered.

The Art of Storytelling in Public Speaking

Picture this: A stage bathed in soft light. An audience hanging on to every word as the speaker weaves an intricate story. The silence is palpable, broken only by the occasional laughter or gasp from the audience. The speaker is not merely relaying facts; they're telling a story, and the audience is completely captivated. This is the art of storytelling in public speaking.

Stories have been central to human communication since time immemorial. They enable us to connect, relate, and empathize. They allow us to transport our listeners into a world of our making. For a public speaker, stories are not just tools, they're secret weapons. A well-told story can hook an audience, keeping them invested and engaged, and can help convey complex ideas in a digestible, relatable way.

So how can you harness the power of storytelling in your speeches? First, remember that every story has a structure: a beginning, a middle, and an end. The beginning should set the stage and engage the listener's attention. The middle should build tension or challenge, and the end should resolve this tension or challenge, leaving the audience with a clear takeaway or lesson.

Next, use vivid, descriptive language. Make your story come alive by painting a picture with your words. Engage your audience's senses. Let them see the colors, smell the aromas, hear the sounds. This not only makes your story more engaging but also more memorable.

Third, make it personal. Personal stories carry emotional weight that resonates with listeners. By sharing something of yourself, you're creating a bond with your audience. They're not just listeners anymore; they're participants in your narrative.

Lastly, keep it relevant. Ensure your story ties in with the overall message of your speech. A story that doesn't support your main points or that strays too far off-topic can confuse your audience and weaken your speech.

Incorporating storytelling into your public speaking repertoire can be a game-changer. It can transform a good speech into a great one. It can turn a passive audience into an engaged one. Master this art, and you'll not only captivate your audience but leave an indelible impression.

Chapter 6: Structure and Flow

Public speaking, like a river, thrives on good structure and a smooth flow. A well-structured speech is akin to a sturdy bridge, guiding your audience from one point to the next with ease and clarity. Flow, on the other hand, is that magic ingredient that makes your speech glide seamlessly, keeping your listeners fully engaged. In Chapter 6, we will delve deep into these two crucial aspects of public speaking: structure and flow.

We will start by understanding how to craft your speech, with a clear beginning, middle, and end. This trio forms the backbone of any effective speech and plays a significant role in helping your audience comprehend and remember your message.

Next, we'll explore the essential techniques for transitioning smoothly between different parts of your speech. The aim is to maintain momentum and ensure your audience stays with you every step of the way.

By mastering the structure and flow of your speeches, you will greatly enhance the impact and persuasiveness of your message. So let's dive in, shall we?

Crafting Your Speech: Beginning, Middle, and End

Speechcraft is an art, a tapestry woven with words and emotions, ideas and pauses, structured meticulously into three distinct segments: the beginning, the middle, and the end. Each of these segments serves a specific purpose and requires careful attention.

The beginning is the attention grabber, the part of your speech that sets the tone and hooks your audience. Picture it as the cover of a book or the entryway into an enchanting garden, beckoning your audience to step in and explore. It is where you introduce your topic, provide a taste of what's to come, and establish a connection with your audience. A well-crafted introduction can stir curiosity, spark interest, and put your listeners on the edge of their seats.

Next is the middle, the heart of your speech, where you deliver the meat of your message. This section should be brimming with well-researched information, compelling arguments, and engaging anecdotes, all pieced together to support your main point or thesis. Think of it as the main course of a meal; it needs to be satisfying and nutritious. Your main points should be clear and distinct, making it easier for your audience to follow along and absorb your message.

Finally, we arrive at the end. The end is your grand finale, where you drive your message home. It is an opportunity for you to summarize the key points, offer a clear takeaway, and close on a high note that leaves a lasting impression. An effective ending could be a powerful call to action, an inspiring quote, or a thought-provoking question. Much like the ending of a memorable movie, your conclusion should encapsulate the essence of your speech and leave your audience with a feeling of fulfillment.

By structuring your speech effectively into a clear beginning, middle, and end, you create a well-organized and captivating narrative that your audience will find easy to follow and hard to forget. But the journey doesn't end here. To ensure a seamless journey for your audience, you need to master the skill of transitioning smoothly from one part of your speech to the next. But we will get to that in the next section. Stay tuned.

Transition Techniques for a Seamless Speech

Now that you've understood the significance of structuring your speech into a beginning, middle, and end, let's delve into the element that binds these segments together into a seamless narrative: transitions.

Consider transitions as bridges that guide your audience from one point to another in your speech. Without these bridges, your audience may get lost in a sea of points, or worse, feel as though they've stumbled upon a sudden cliffhanger. Transition techniques help maintain the flow of your speech, ensuring that your audience can follow your narrative journey smoothly.

There are several techniques you can employ to create effective transitions.

Firstly, preview and review are fundamental tools. At the end of one point, preview what's coming next. This might sound as simple as, "Having explored the causes, let's now turn our attention to the potential solutions." When you begin the next point, review the previous one briefly to provide context, such as, "We've discussed the causes, and it's clear we need effective solutions, so let's explore what those might be."

Secondly, make use of signpost words and phrases. These verbal cues act as traffic signs on the highway of your speech, guiding your audience on the journey. Phrases like "firstly," "moving on," "in contrast," "additionally," act as clear indicators of where you're headed.

Thirdly, use repetition and parallelism. Repeating a keyword or phrase links ideas and makes them more memorable. Parallelism, using similar structures for related points, provides a rhythm that enhances comprehension.

Finally, consider creating a thematic link. By weaving a theme, an anecdote, or a metaphor throughout your speech, you create a thread that your audience can follow from start to finish. This technique requires finesse but can produce a powerful, cohesive speech when done well.

Transitions, when crafted effectively, can guide your audience through your speech as effortlessly as a well-guided tour. They ensure that your audience doesn't miss any important sights along the way and makes the journey enjoyable and memorable. Now, with a well-structured speech and seamless transitions in your arsenal, let's explore some practical tools and techniques to further enhance your public speaking prowess. But that's a tale for the next chapter.

Chapter 7: Practical Tools and Techniques

Public speaking, like any fine art, involves an intricate balance of theoretical knowledge and practical skill. We've journeyed through the realms of fear, voice, audience, nonverbal and verbal communication, and finally structure and flow. Now, let's roll up our sleeves and dive into the more practical aspects of public speaking. We will explore two critical areas that can help you control your delivery and maintain your composure, namely breathing and voice projection techniques, and practical exercises to cope with stage fright. These tools and techniques will serve as your personal toolbox, ever ready to help you build a stronger foundation and fortify your public speaking castle. Let's dig in.

Breathing and Voice Projection Techniques

Breathing techniques form the bedrock of effective speech delivery. A well-regulated breath not only calms the nerves, but also powers your voice, giving it the strength to reach the back of the room and the gentleness to evoke emotions in your listeners. Deep, diaphragmatic breathing is a skill worth mastering. This involves breathing deeply into your diaphragm, not shallowly into your chest, enabling you to access your full vocal range and power. We'll cover some exercises that can help you cultivate this deep breathing habit, such as the box breathing technique, where you inhale, hold, exhale, and hold each for a count of four.

Next, let's talk about voice projection. Consider the space you're speaking in, the size of the audience, the acoustics of the room. All these factors play into how much you need to project your voice. But remember, projection is not shouting. It's about using your diaphragm and breath to fuel your voice's volume and resonance, helping it travel farther. It's the art of speaking to a person at the back of the room as though they were right in front of you. Techniques such as forward placement, where you try to resonate your voice in the mask of your face (the area around your nose and mouth), can help you project without straining your vocal cords.

Developing a rich, powerful, resonant voice takes practice. To help you on this journey, we'll cover some simple yet powerful exercises. For instance, the "Straw Technique" can help you strengthen your voice and increase your breath control. By regularly practicing voice projection, you can ensure that every person in your audience, whether they're sitting in the first row or the last, hears your message loud and clear.

Breathing and voice projection are more than just technical skills; they're your lifelines in public speaking. By mastering these techniques, you can control your speech delivery, reduce anxiety, and deliver your message with confidence and clarity. So, take a deep breath, and let's dive into the techniques that will give your voice wings.

Coping with Stage Fright: Practical Exercises

The dry mouth, the sweaty palms, the butterflies pirouetting in your stomach—yes, we're talking about stage fright. It's a common phenomenon, almost a rite of passage for anyone who steps onto the stage. But, don't let that deter you. The fact is, even the most experienced speakers feel a flutter of nerves before a presentation. The trick is to harness this energy to enhance, not hinder, your performance.

One of the most powerful weapons to combat stage fright is preparation. Familiarity breeds confidence. The more familiar you are with your material, the less room there is for anxiety. Start by rehearsing your speech, preferably in the venue you'll be speaking at. Understand the space, the acoustics, the vibe. The more at home you feel, the less intimidating the environment will be.

Visualization is another potent tool. Close your eyes, breathe deeply, and imagine delivering a successful speech. Visualize the audience's reaction, the applause, the sense of satisfaction. By regularly practicing this, you can condition your mind to associate public speaking with positive experiences, reducing the fear factor.

Physical exercises can also be a game-changer in managing stage fright. For instance, practicing mindfulness and yoga can help center your mind, reduce anxiety, and improve focus. Even a quick warm-up before you step onto the stage, such as stretching or doing a couple of deep-breathing exercises, can help calm your nerves and get the adrenaline flowing in a controlled manner.

Remember the wise words of Mark Twain, "Do the thing you fear the most, and the death of fear is certain." In the spirit of this advice, consider joining a local public speaking group or seeking opportunities to speak in public. With every speech, you'll find your fear diminishing and your confidence growing.

Coping with stage fright isn't about eradicating fear—it's about mastering it. It's about transforming those butterflies in your stomach into a flight formation that propels you to new heights of public speaking. The exercises shared in this section are your stepping stones on this journey. Remember, every great speaker was once a beginner. So, go on, step onto that stage, and let the world hear your voice.

Chapter 8:
The Power of Practice

We have travelled quite a journey in our exploration of public speaking, haven't we? We've unraveled the intricacies of fear, the significance of voice, the essence of knowing your audience, the impact of nonverbal and verbal communication, the importance of structure, and we've even armed ourselves with practical tools to master this art form. Now, we're onto a vital component that binds all of these together: practice.

As Aristotle once said, "We are what we repeatedly do. Excellence, then, is not an act, but a habit." This rings especially true when it comes to public speaking. It is through the power of practice that we engrain the skills we've learned so far, turning them from a set of techniques to an innate part of our communicative identity.

In this chapter, we shall delve into the realm of practice—how to practice effectively, and how to use feedback to facilitate continual improvement. Each word spoken, each gesture made, and each pause taken is an opportunity to refine your public speaking abilities. So, let's seize these opportunities and sculpt ourselves into the eloquent speakers we aspire to be.

How to Practice Effectively: Techniques and Tips

Practice. A seemingly simple word that holds the key to unlocking your potential in public speaking. But how does one practice effectively? Is it simply a matter of repetition, or is there more to it? Allow me to take you through the various techniques and tips that can elevate your practice sessions from mundane to highly productive.

First off, remember that effective practice is deliberate. It's not just about repeating the same speech over and over again. It involves setting clear, achievable goals. Maybe today you focus on your vocal variety, tomorrow you work on eliminating filler words, and the next day, you concentrate on your nonverbal cues. Each practice session should have a specific objective.

Once you've decided your focus, it's time to get down to business. And by business, I mean practice in an environment that mimics the actual situation as closely as possible. If you'll be delivering your speech on a stage, find an open space to practice. If you'll be using a microphone, get your hands on one. This is all about acclimatizing yourself to the actual conditions to minimize surprises.

Now let's talk about a method which can provide you an insight like no other - recording yourself. Audio or video, it doesn't matter. What matters is that when you review the recording, you become both the speaker and the audience. You see what they see, hear what they hear. This can be an eye-opener in terms of identifying areas for improvement.

Remember, though, that you are not aiming for perfection. Instead, you are striving for progress. It's essential to forgive yourself for the mistakes you make during practice. They are opportunities for learning, not anchors to hold you back.

Repetition is, of course, a critical part of practice. However, it's important to avoid mindless repetition. Every time you rehearse your speech, do it with full intent, as if you were delivering it to your audience. This will not only help you engrain the content better but will also build your confidence.

Lastly, consider using the sandwich technique during your practice sessions. Begin by visualizing a successful speech delivery, then practice your speech, focusing on your identified goal, and end by once again visualizing a successful speech. This method helps condition your mind towards success and positivity.

As you navigate your journey through public speaking, remember the old adage, "practice makes perfect". In our case, though, let's amend that to "practice makes progress". Keep your eye on the progress, not perfection. After all, public speaking is a skill that one can always enhance, no matter how experienced they are. With these techniques and tips in your practice toolbox, you are well on your way to mastering the art of public speaking.

Using Feedback for Improvement

Feedback. It's the secret ingredient that can give your public speaking skills a real edge. However, the art of using feedback effectively is not as straightforward as it might seem. It requires an open mind, a receptive attitude, and the courage to face your shortcomings head-on. Let's dive into how you can use feedback to refine your public speaking abilities.

Let's start with the source of feedback. Ideally, you want feedback from a variety of sources. This can range from a mentor or coach who has expertise in public speaking, to your peers, and even the audience you speak to. Each one can offer a unique perspective that can help you improve.

Once you've received the feedback, the next step is to process it. At this stage, it's crucial to remember that feedback, even when it's critical, is not personal. It's about the speech, not you. Maintaining this mindset can help you approach the feedback more objectively.

While processing feedback, look for patterns. If multiple people mention that you speak too quickly, for instance, that's a clear sign that you need to work on your pace. Individual comments can be helpful, but patterns in feedback can point out fundamental areas for improvement.

When it comes to putting feedback into action, be selective. Trying to change everything all at once can be overwhelming and counterproductive. Instead, pick one or two key pieces of feedback that you believe will have the most impact on your speech and focus on those first.

As you make changes based on the feedback, it's important to gauge the effect of these changes. This is where more feedback comes in. If you've worked on slowing down your speech based on feedback and your audience now finds your pace comfortable, you know you've made effective use of the feedback.

Keep in mind that not all feedback will be useful, and that's okay. Some of it might be contradictory, and some might not align with your speaking style or objectives. The trick is to distill from the feedback what will truly help you grow as a speaker.

Lastly, remember to thank people for their feedback. Encouraging feedback creates a supportive environment for your growth. A simple thank you can go a long way in maintaining open lines of communication.

In the realm of public speaking, feedback is not just about identifying what you're doing wrong. It's also about recognizing what you're doing right. So, seek feedback, absorb it, and use it. This ongoing cycle of feedback and improvement is what will propel you from a good speaker to a great one. Remember, every piece of feedback is a stepping stone on your path to mastering public speaking.

Chapter 9: Conquering Different Speaking Scenarios

Speaking in public comes in many flavors - some sweet, some bitter, and some a complex blend of both. A well-rehearsed business presentation, an impromptu speech at a friend's birthday, or a toast at a wedding, each scenario presents its own challenges and opportunities. In this chapter, we will explore various speaking scenarios, each one requiring its own set of skills and nuances. You'll learn how to handle off-the-cuff speeches with aplomb, enhance your presentation skills for the professional world, and master the art of delivering a toast that can tug at heartstrings or prompt a hearty laugh. By the end of this chapter, you'll have the tools you need to face different speaking situations with confidence and charisma.

Impromptu Speeches: Thinking on Your Feet

The spotlight hits you. Someone hands you a microphone. A room full of eyes look expectantly at you. You were just asked to say a few words and you didn't see it coming. Welcome to the exhilarating world of impromptu speeches! Despite the surprise, with the right skills, you can turn this challenging situation into an opportunity to shine.

An impromptu speech, by definition, is one that is unplanned or unprepared. The unpredictability might seem intimidating, but it's important to realize that this is not a test of your preparedness, but a test of your adaptability. Remember that the audience is aware you're speaking on the spur of the moment and will generally be more forgiving of minor fumbles.

Your first and foremost ally in such situations is your ability to stay calm. Keeping a cool head not only helps you think clearly but also projects confidence to your audience. If you're feeling a surge of adrenaline, channel it into enthusiasm for your subject.

Second, organize your thoughts quickly into a simple structure. The 'Point, Reason, Example, Point' (PREP) method is particularly handy. Start with the main point you want to make (P), explain the reason (R) why you hold that point, illustrate it with an example (E), and then recap the point (P) you are making. This framework provides a clear and concise way for you to articulate your thoughts and ensures your message comes across effectively.

Active listening is another crucial skill for impromptu speeches. If you're responding to someone else or continuing a dialogue, ensure you're building on what's been said before. It shows respect for your colleagues' contributions and provides a logical starting point for your speech.

Also, don't shy away from using personal stories. They don't just make your speech more relatable but are also easier for you to recount under pressure. However, always remember to tie it back to the main point you're making.

Even in the world of impromptu speeches, practice has its place. Seize opportunities to speak off-the-cuff, be it during team meetings, at social events, or even by joining a local Toastmasters club. It's through regular practice that the art of thinking on your feet becomes second nature.

And finally, remember that brevity is your friend. When you're speaking without a script, it's easy to ramble or go off on a tangent. Keep your speech short and focused, and end decisively. It's better to make a single point well than to skim over several topics.

Impromptu speaking can feel like navigating a labyrinth in the dark. But with these tips in your arsenal, you'll be ready to take it head-on, finding your way through with confidence, poise, and even a bit of flair.

Presentation Skills for the Workplace

The ability to effectively communicate ideas and concepts is a priceless asset in the professional world. Workplace presentations, whether they're for pitching a new project, explaining a business strategy, or leading a team meeting, often hold a significant weight in shaping your career trajectory. Mastering these situations can be your ladder to greater opportunities, and here's how you can do it.

For starters, knowing your audience is essential. Who are they? What's their level of knowledge about your topic? Are they colleagues from your department, or are they higher-ups in the company? Answering these questions will help you tailor your content and presentation style to your audience, making your message more impactful.

Keep your presentation purpose clear and focused. It's easy to get lost in a sea of data and facts, so remember that less is often more. Hone in on your main points and make them the stars of your presentation. Think of your presentation as a narrative - there should be a compelling beginning, a substantial middle, and a clear conclusion. Every point you make should serve to drive your narrative forward.

Visual aids can be powerful tools, but they should enhance your message, not distract from it. If you're using slides, don't clutter them with text. Use images, infographics, and diagrams wherever possible. Remember, your slides are there to support you, not to replace you as the presenter.

The way you deliver your presentation is just as important as the content itself. Practice good body language. Stand tall, make eye contact, and use open gestures. These non-verbal cues can greatly influence how your audience perceives you and your message.

Work on your vocal delivery as well. Ensure your voice is loud and clear enough to be heard at the back of the room. Vary your tone and pace to keep your audience engaged. A monotone delivery can make even the most exciting content seem dull.

Preparation is key. Make sure you know your material inside and out. This will not only boost your confidence but also allow you to handle any unexpected issues or questions that may come up. Remember to rehearse your presentation several times before the actual day.

Finally, engage with your audience. Encourage questions and feedback. Interaction keeps your audience involved and makes your presentation more memorable. Don't be afraid to show your passion and enthusiasm for your topic. If you're excited about your presentation, your audience will be too.

Workplace presentations don't have to be a source of anxiety. With a clear focus, effective delivery, and thorough preparation, you can seize these moments to showcase your expertise, share your ideas, and make a positive impact on your career.

Giving a Toast: Weddings, Birthdays, and More

On a joyous occasion such as a wedding, a birthday, an anniversary, or a retirement party, you may find yourself given the honor of making a toast. Even if it's not your typical boardroom or conference stage, these scenarios are prime opportunities to showcase your public speaking prowess. Here's how you can make your toast the highlight of the event.

To start, remember that your toast is not about you. It's about the person or people being celebrated. Make them the focus of your toast. Share anecdotes or stories about them, speak about their achievements, and express your heartfelt wishes for them.

Being brief and to the point is key. A toast is not a lengthy speech. Aim for two to three minutes. Anything longer might risk losing your audience's attention. The beauty of a toast lies in its conciseness. You're not trying to narrate a biography, but to capture the essence of a moment.

Preparation is just as important for a toast as it is for any other speech. Jot down what you want to say and practice it. This will help you get the pacing right and ensure you're not rambling. Remember, confidence is borne from preparation, and a confident toast is a successful toast.

Humor can be a wonderful element in a toast, but use it wisely. Light-hearted stories or jokes that evoke a shared memory are usually safe bets. Avoid any humor that could potentially embarrass or hurt anyone. The aim is to celebrate, not to roast.

When you're delivering your toast, let your sincerity shine through. This is not a formal presentation where you need to maintain a strict professional demeanor. It's okay to show emotion, to let your voice waver a bit if you're moved. Genuine emotion can make your toast more powerful and memorable.

Begin and end your toast on a high note. Start with a brief introduction about yourself and your relationship with the person you're toasting to. This sets the context for your audience. Conclude your toast with a clear, definitive statement, something that leaves no doubt that your toast has ended. This could be a traditional toast phrase, a quote, or simply a heartfelt wish for the person or people being celebrated.

Finally, practice the mechanics of the toast. If you're holding a glass, make sure you're comfortable with it. Know when you're expected to raise the glass and when to drink. These might seem like minor details, but you'd be surprised how often people get flustered by them.

Giving a toast is an honor and a responsibility. But with a little preparation, sincerity, and tact, it can be a delightful experience, a moment that you and the celebrants will treasure for years to come.

Chapter 10: Advanced Public Speaking Strategies

Having built a robust foundation in the art of public speaking, we now turn our attention to some advanced strategies that can make your speeches more engaging, persuasive, and memorable. This chapter will explore the utility of rhetorical devices, providing you with a toolkit to enrich your language and captivate your audience. We will also delve into the realm of persuasive speaking, where you will learn about ethos, pathos, and logos, the classic triumvirate of rhetorical appeal. Through this knowledge, you will unlock a new level of influence, ensuring your speeches have not just style, but also substance. Strap yourself in; we're about to dive deep into the nuanced world of rhetorical prowess.

Utilizing Rhetorical Devices

You've now reached a stage where you can effectively articulate your ideas, establish rapport with your audience, and even control those pesky nerves. The next step is to embellish your speeches, adding an extra layer of eloquence and impact to your words. This is where rhetorical devices come into play, offering a panoply of options to take your speech from good to great.

Anaphora, for instance, is a useful tool that involves repeating a certain phrase at the beginning of consecutive clauses or sentences. This device can be used to emphasize key points and elicit a certain emotional response from your audience. Politicians, poets, and other eloquent speakers frequently employ this device to remarkable effect.

Metaphors and similes, often grouped under the umbrella of 'figurative language,' are another pair of devices at your disposal. By equating an abstract concept with a familiar image, you can illuminate complex ideas and tap into the imaginative faculties of your audience. Figurative language can make your speech more engaging and memorable.

Then, there's the rule of three. The human mind is adept at grasping things in threes, which is why many great speeches and slogans incorporate this device. Just think about 'Life, Liberty, and the Pursuit of Happiness.' The rule of three can make your speeches more rhythmic, persuasive, and memorable.

Parallelism, much like the rule of three, relies on the repetition of grammatical structures to create rhythm and emphasis. For instance, consider the phrase, 'I came, I saw, I conquered.' The repeated structure not only creates a rhythm but also amplifies the speaker's accomplishments.

Rhetorical questions can also be powerful tools in your arsenal. By posing a question that doesn't require a response, you can stimulate your audience's thought process and subtly guide them towards your desired conclusion.

Remember, while these devices can enhance your speech, they must be used judiciously. Overuse can lead to a speech sounding contrived or overly dramatic. Aim for balance, subtly weaving these devices into your speech to enhance its impact without distracting from your core message.

Think of these rhetorical devices as the seasoning to a dish. They don't replace the need for high-quality ingredients (i.e., strong content and a clear structure), but they can certainly elevate the overall flavor. Use them wisely, and you'll take your public speaking skills to a whole new level.

The Power of Persuasion: Ethos, Pathos, and Logos

We've made a remarkable journey together, from understanding our fears to presenting effectively in various scenarios. Now, we're stepping into the world of persuasion, where we'll encounter three formidable allies – ethos, pathos, and logos. Together, they form the triad of persuasive appeals, as coined by Aristotle. Utilizing these can significantly boost the impact and persuasiveness of your public speaking.

Let's begin with ethos, which refers to ethical appeal. It's about establishing your credibility and trustworthiness as a speaker. How can you achieve this? By showcasing your knowledge and experience, or through your demeanor and the way you articulate your points. Listeners are more likely to be persuaded by a speaker they perceive as credible and trustworthy.

Pathos, on the other hand, taps into the emotions of your audience. Emotional appeal can be a powerful driver of decision making and opinion formation. But remember, this is not about emotional manipulation; it's about understanding your audience's feelings and perspectives, and aligning your message with them. Stories, anecdotes, and expressive language are some ways to stir emotions in your audience.

Finally, we have logos, or logical appeal. This involves using reasoning, evidence, facts, and logical arguments to persuade your audience. When your arguments are solid and your facts are verifiable, you stand a better chance of swaying your audience.

To illustrate these concepts, let's consider a scenario. Suppose you're giving a speech advocating for environmental conservation. You could use ethos by mentioning your background in environmental science, pathos by sharing heart-wrenching stories of wildlife affected by pollution, and logos by presenting statistics showing the rate of deforestation and its impact on global warming.

However, the trick lies in using a balanced combination of ethos, pathos, and logos, as over-reliance on one can weaken your overall argument. For instance, relying too heavily on emotional appeal might make your argument seem less rational, while overusing logical appeal could potentially bore your audience.

Remember, public speaking is not just about conveying information; it's about persuading your audience to consider a new perspective or spur them into action. By mastering ethos, pathos, and logos, you'll be well on your way to achieving this goal. At the end of the day, a powerful speaker is not just heard, but also remembered and followed. It's time for you to become one.

Conclusion

Here we are, my friends, at the culmination of our journey. This is not an end, rather the beginning of your exciting voyage into the world of public speaking. We have covered an expanse of ground, from confronting and overcoming speech anxiety, through the intricacies of verbal and nonverbal communication, to the art of storytelling, and even into the realm of advanced strategies such as rhetorical devices and the powerful trio of ethos, pathos, and logos. This final chapter, the conclusion, brings us to two pivotal cornerstones – Becoming a Lifelong Learner in Public Speaking and Your Next Steps: Putting It All into Practice. Remember, the most effective public speakers are not those who rest on their laurels, but those who continually strive to learn and improve. Let's move forward with the same enthusiasm with which we started, and keep the spirit of learning alive.

Becoming a Lifelong Learner in Public Speaking

Public speaking, like any other skill, thrives on continuous learning and improvement. It's a journey, not a destination. The most influential speakers are those who never stop evolving, refining their craft with every opportunity they get. You might be wondering, "I've covered all the chapters in this book, what's next?" This is exactly the attitude that primes you for lifelong learning.

Understanding that there is always room for improvement is crucial. No matter how seasoned a speaker you become, there will always be ways to sharpen your communication skills and become more effective at conveying your ideas. Even the most renowned speakers were not born with innate eloquence. They dedicated their lives to learning and honing their craft, continuously seeking ways to grow and improve.

Encourage yourself to be curious and open to new knowledge and experiences. This is the essence of lifelong learning. It could be as simple as learning a new word each day, reading extensively, or staying updated on current events. Engaging with diverse forms of content exposes you to different perspectives and broadens your thinking, enriching your speeches.

Joining public speaking groups or organizations can also offer platforms for continuous learning. These communities provide opportunities for regular practice, constructive feedback, and learning from other speakers. It's an environment that encourages experimentation and growth, promoting the spirit of lifelong learning.

Attending workshops, seminars, or courses in public speaking can further enhance your skills. These provide an avenue to delve into specific areas you wish to improve, whether it's storytelling, voice modulation, body language, or persuasive techniques. They offer you an opportunity to learn from experts in the field, gain valuable insights, and push your boundaries.

Finally, being receptive to feedback is vital. Treat each critique as an opportunity to learn and evolve. No matter how small or large the audience, there's always something to be gleaned from their reactions. Use this to adapt and refine your speech delivery for future performances.

Remember, the most successful public speakers are not those who have reached a certain level and stopped. They are those who view every speaking opportunity as a chance to learn, to experiment, and to grow. As you step into the world of public speaking, wear the hat of a lifelong learner, and remember that every step you take is progress on your journey. The aim is not to be perfect, but to be a little better each time you stand behind that podium.

Your Next Steps: Putting It All into Practice

Having covered the breadth and depth of public speaking in the preceding chapters, it's now time to take the crucial next steps. Remember, public speaking is a practical skill, best learned and honed through consistent practice. This section will guide you on how to take your newly acquired knowledge and skills from theory to practice.

First, get out there and start speaking. Find opportunities to speak in public. Volunteer to make presentations at work, propose a toast at a social gathering, or participate in local speaking clubs. The goal here is to gain practical experience, which is the best way to consolidate and apply your learning.

Second, make it a habit to review your performances. Recording your speeches can be incredibly helpful for this. Watch the recordings and look out for areas of improvement. Are you using appropriate body language? Is your voice clear and modulated?

Are your arguments well structured and persuasive? Self-evaluation is an effective way to keep refining your skills.

Third, invite feedback from others. It could be from your colleagues, friends, or fellow members of your speaking club. Constructive criticism can offer valuable insights into how your message is perceived, and how effectively you are communicating. Be open to this feedback and use it as a tool for improvement.

Fourth, always be ready to adapt and improve. Remember, every public speaking engagement is different. Be prepared to tailor your approach depending on your audience, the context, and the purpose of your speech. Versatility is a valuable asset in public speaking.

Fifth, don't forget to prepare. Even as you become more comfortable with public speaking, the importance of preparation should not be underestimated. Remember the saying: "The only place where success comes before work is in the dictionary."

Sixth, continue learning. Even after you've become proficient, never stop seeking knowledge and ways to improve your skills. Attend workshops, read books, watch speeches by experienced speakers, and stay abreast of developments in the field of public speaking.

Finally, keep the spirit of public speaking alive. Remember that at the heart of public speaking is the desire to share a message, to communicate effectively, and to impact your audience in some way. Hold on to that passion and let it guide your journey in public speaking.

Your journey in mastering public speaking doesn't end with the last page of this book. Instead, it's just the beginning. With continuous practice, self-evaluation, and an open mind, you're on your way to becoming a truly effective public speaker. Take these next steps, put it all into practice, and witness your transformation unfold.

About the Author

Hello there, I'm Richard Bell. A public speaking enthusiast, educated in the intertwined fields of speech communication and psychology, and above all, a lifelong learner.

My journey with public speaking began early in life, a natural storyteller with a penchant for captivating audiences. Over the years, I've honed this skill, expanding my abilities from the simple art of captivating narratives to the complex strategies of persuasive speaking, communication psychology, and public engagement. But my academic background isn't what defines me entirely as a speaker, it's the shared human experiences, the collective sighs, laughs, and nods from the audience that truly make the whole process worthwhile.

On a more personal note, I share my life with a wonderful family - my wife, our children, and Sunny, our lively dog who's always up for an adventure. When I'm not immersed in the world of public speaking or family duties, you'll likely find me outdoors. Nature is my sanctuary and I find hiking and biking are great ways to both explore it and keep myself physically active. These activities not only bring me joy, but they serve as a refreshing break from the hustle and bustle of everyday life, and often, a source of inspiration for my next big speech.

So, as we embark on this journey together, know that we are learning from each other. The experiences I share in this book come from not just my personal and professional life but also my acquired knowledge. I hope to guide you as you navigate the fascinating world of public speaking, helping you uncover your strengths, improve your weaknesses, and ultimately, empower you to voice out your ideas confidently and authentically.